THE MYSTERY
OF THE
LOOKING GLASS

JOHN MARINELLI

TABLE OF CONTENTS

PREFACE

I chose to write on this subject because it teaches the truth of the gospel in that the human spirit was and should now be a reflection of Jesus. When others look at us, they should see God. We should be his reflection.

Most Christians do not see this truth and do not seek to bring it into reality. They instead, look to see themselves and seek to improve that image as they live from day to day.

The scriptures teach that we are to be the reflection of Jesus In this world. We will discuss the concept of being a reflection: why? How, When, Hindrances, Benefits, and much more.

INTRODUCTION

Here is what the apostle Paul wrote to the church at Corinth in the first century. This is the 3rd chapter of II Corinthians.

2. Ye are our epistle written in our hearts, known and read of all men:

(It was common in those days to carry a letter of recommendation when visiting a new church. The practice was established because false teachers would show up and say, "Paul or Peter sent me" The letter stopped this deception.)

3. Forasmuch as ye are manifestly declared to be the epistle of Christ ministered by us, written not with ink, but with the Spirit of The living God; not in tables of stone, but in fleshy tables of the heart.

(Paul tells the church that a letter of recommendation is not necessary for them because they are his letter by their service to God when he led them to Christ.)

4. And such trust have we through Christ to God-ward:

5. Not that we are sufficient of ourselves to think anything as of ourselves; but our sufficiency is of God;

6. Who also has made us able ministers of the new testament; not of the letter, but of the spirit: for the letter kills, but the spirit gives life.

(Paul now switches the meaning of the letter from a recommendation to the Law of Moses, saying the letter kills, but the Spirit brings life.)

7. But if the ministration of death, written and engraved in stones, was glorious, so that the children of Israel could not steadfastly behold the face of Moses for the glory of his countenance; which glory was to be done away:

(Paul again refers to the law as a ministry of death, yet it had its own glory. Death is used because we could not keep the law and the penalty is death. The glory is because God was in it from the beginning and his justice was being fulfilled. This glory was evident in the face of Moses as he descended from the mountain. Paul says that even though it was glorious, it would be done away with making room for God's grace.)

8. How shall not the ministration of the spirit be rather glorious?

9. For if the ministration of condemnation be glory, much more doth the ministration of righteousness exceeds in glory.

(Note the comparison between the condemnation of the law and the ministration of righteousness. The old must give way to the new and the glory of the new exceeds the glory of the old.)

10. For even that which was made glorious had no glory in this respect, by reason of the glory that excels.

11. For if that which is done away was glorious, much more that which remains is glorious.

12. Seeing then that we have such hope, we use great plainness of speech:

13. And not as Moses, which put a veil over his face, that the children of Israel could not steadfastly look to the end of that which is abolished:

(The veil is given to hide the glory of the law so the ones looking at it would not see its end, which was death.)

14. But their minds were blinded: for until this day remains the same veil, untaken away, in the reading of the old testament; which veil is done away in Christ.

(Chapter 4:1-2 says the veil remains because of the hidden things of dishonesty. Verse 16 says when they turn unto the Lord, the veil will be removed. As for us, the veil was taken away in Christ.)

15. But even unto this day, when Moses is read, the veil is upon their heart.

(The veil started as a covering over Moses's face to hide the glory of God. Now, Paul tells us that it is a covering over the heart to hide the glory of God from the disobedient.)

16. Nevertheless when it shall turn to the Lord, the veil shall be taken away.

(Repentance is all that is needed to remove the veil)

17. Now the Lord is that Spirit: and where the Spirit of the Lord is, there is liberty.

(Liberty from what? The obvious conclusion is the condemnation of the Law. It is the Spirit that supersedes the death of sin to bring forth life and grace in the lives of those who repent.)

18. But we all, with open face beholding as in a glass (Mirror) the glory of the Lord, are changed into the same image from glory to glory, even as by the Spirit of the Lord.

(An "open face" is a clean conscience and a transparent heart.)

I Corinthians 4:1-2..."Therefore, seeing we have this ministry, as we have received mercy, we faint not; But have renounced the hidden things of dishonesty, not walking in craftiness, nor handling the word of God deceitfully; but by manifestation of the truth commending ourselves to every man's conscience in the sight of God."

(As we receive mercy from God because of our repentance, we do not faint in the presence of God's glory. Instead, we begin to handle the word of God honestly and make know its truth in our world. The mystery of looking into the looking glass or mirror… "with open face beholding as ***in a glass*** the glory of the Lord, is that we are changed into the same image from glory to glory, even as by the Spirit of the Lord". This is a mystery…to be the reflection of Jesus.

Paul is comparing the law, written in the ten commandments, to the grace of God. Both contained the glory of God. However, the old testament saints could not look upon its glory because they operated in the flesh and held onto dishonesty.

Read again verse 14. "But have renounced the hidden things of dishonesty, not walking in craftiness, nor handling the word of God deceitfully.

The New Testament saints renounced the hidden things of dishonesty and were standing with a clear conscience or "Open Face".

Verse 14 also tells us that the veil that covers the minds of those that do not believe, in this case, the Jews will be taken away by Christ when they turn to him.

We can see the end of things whereas they cannot because of their dishonesty. We can behold the glory of the Lord as though we were standing in his presence, and where others would faint, we receive mercy and stand before him rejoicing.

We are privileged to look into the face of the Lord. When we do, we are changed into his likeness and linage.

CHAPTER ONE:
THE NEED FOR CHANGE

It all happened with Adam. He and Eve became disobedient to God, their creator. They were made to be a reflection of God in the earth. They were created to have fellowship with God on his level. All this is found in Romans 5:12 ff.

Their innocence was turned into evil, and they fell from their consistent union with God. The full story is in Genesis, chapter two. Their rebellion caused their spiritual death. They knew the decree made by God about the day they ate of the tree of the knowledge of good and evil, that they would surely die. They ignored it and bought the lie that they could be like God.

God never wanted man to know evil. He was created to be holy. Knowing evil put them on a path to be their own gods. But it did not include the image and likeness of God, as they were originally fashioned. Instead, they became servants unto sin and their God-like personalities vanished. They now were stuck with the nature of evil, the very personality of Satan, who deceived them in the first place.

Romans 5:12 tells us that death passed upon all men, for all have sinned. Man became separated from God and dead in his own sin. This is why there is a need for change.

To restore the image of God, man had to first be freed from his sin. Then the transformation could take place. This is why Jesus died on the cross. His death paid the penalty for our sin and his life gave us salvation. Romans 10:9-10.

Now, we can come to God with an "Open Face." As we look into the looking glass, we can behold Jesus and watch as the Spirit of the living God changes us from one glorious encounter to another.

Instead of manifesting jealousy, hate, pride, murder, immorality and all the rest of the deeds of the flesh, as recorded in Galatians 5:22ff, we gradually manifest the fruit of the Spirit. This will become our new personality, fashioned after God in righteousness and true holiness.

The Bible refers to this change as being "Born Again." However, many Christians do not profess to be born again. (PEW Reports)"

Why should I be "Born Again?" After all, over 50% of American Christians are not. They go to church and even practice their religion faithfully. They are, for the most part, good people.

Paul tells us in his letter to the Roman Christians in the 1st century what went wrong and how to fix it. He said, (5:12)

"Wherefore, as by one man sin entered into the world, and death by sin; and so death passed upon all men, for that all have sinned: (5:14) (For until the law sin was in the world: but sin is not imputed when there is no law.

Nevertheless, death reigned from Adam to Moses, even over them that had not sinned after the similitude of Adam's transgression, who is the figure of him that was to come. (5:17)

For if by one man's offence death reigned by one; much more they which receive abundance of grace and of the gift of righteousness shall reign in life by one, Jesus Christ.) (5:21) That as sin has reigned unto death, even so might grace reign through righteousness unto eternal life by Jesus Christ our Lord."

I should be born again so I can become the new creature God has planned for me; so I can become a child of God; so I can dwell in his presence for all eternity; so I can finally be free from the sin that plagues my soul day and night; so I can have fellowship with my Heavenly Father.

However, the main reason for us to be "Born Again" is because it is our divine destiny. It is the will of God. It is the only way we will see heaven, Jesus, and all the saints. This is the pathway to God, the Father.

Being **"Born Again"** holds significant spiritual and personal benefits for believers. Let's explore some of these:

Salvation and Eternal Life: The primary benefit is **salvation**. When a person is "Born Again" through faith in Jesus Christ, they receive forgiveness for their sins and the promise of **eternal life.** This new birth marks the beginning of a transformed relationship with God.

Spiritual Transformation: Being "Born Again" involves a **spiritual rebirth**. The Holy Spirit indwells the believer, empowering them to live a life that reflects God's character. Old habits and sinful patterns are replaced by new desires and godly attitudes.

New Identity: Through the new birth, believers receive a **new identity**. They become children of God, adopted into his family. Their status changes from being spiritually dead to being alive in Christ.

Freedom From Bondage: "Born Again" believers experience freedom from the bondage of sin. The power of sin is broken, and they can overcome temptations with the Holy Spirit's guidance.

Purpose and Calling: God has a unique purpose for each believer. Being "Born Again" opens the door to discovering and fulfilling that purpose. Believers are called to serve God and others, using their gifts and talents for his glory.

Assurance of God's Love: The new birth assures believers of God's unwavering love. They know that nothing can separate them from his love (Romans 8:38-39).

Fellowship With Other Believers: "Born Again" Christians become part of the global family of believers. They find fellowship, encouragement, and support from other followers.

Hope And Joy: The hope of eternal life and the joy of knowing Christ bring deep satisfaction. "Born Again" believers experience a sense of purpose and fulfillment that transcends earthly circumstances.

Being **"Born Again"** is not a mere ritual; it is a profound transformation of the heart and soul. Jesus emphasized this truth when he said, "Truly, truly, I say to you, unless one is "Born Again", he cannot see the kingdom of God" (John 3:3, ESV). It is an invitation to experience God's grace and enter a new life in Christ.

There is a metaphor seen in nature that depicts this experience. It is the butterfly. As you may know, the butterfly undergoes a miraculous transformation from a caterpillar into an entirely new creature. So it is with the human soul. It undergoes a transformation from evil to righteous; from darkness to light; from death to life.

I wrote this poem a while back.

Be A Butterfly

Be a Butterfly
And fly away with me.
We'll fly on God's Promises
Right into eternity.

Be a Butterfly
To crawl no more.
But to soar in the Spirit
Above earth's mighty roar.

Be a Butterfly
To fly to heights unknown.
Soaring on the wings of faith
Never more to be alone.

Be a Butterfly
And fly away with me.
For God has made us new
At last! At last! We are free.

Written by
John Marinelli

The butterfly is a great example of the process of change that happens to our hearts when we put away deceitfulness and gaze into the looking glass (God's Holy Bible).

Change is essential for moving on with God. He does not entertain evil, which is woven into the fabric of man. He invites us to change and grow in his grace so we can walk on his level and experience fellowship with him. Listen to what Paul said to the church in Rome.

"I beseech you therefore, brethren, by the mercies of God, that ye present your bodies a living sacrifice, holy, acceptable unto God, which is your reasonable service. And be not conformed to this world: but be ye transformed by the renewing of your mind, that ye may prove what is that good, and acceptable, and perfect, will of God." Romans 12:1-2.

There's that "change" word again…be transformed. It is what God wants, and we are called to a destiny of change.

The true follower of Christ will want to be changed and will submit to the transformation process. He or she wants to be in the presence of God and enjoy his blessings. The rebellious and fake Christians will remain as they are, their own gods, with themselves on the throne of their lives.

Being "Born Again" begins with God. He draws us to himself. (John 6:44) Jesus said, "no one can come to me unless the Father who sent me draws him, and I will raise him up at the last day."

However, the call to salvation is an open invitation to all who believe. John 3:16 tells us,

"For God so loved the world, that he gave his only begotten Son, that whosoever believeth in him should not perish, but have everlasting life." The whosoever is called. God is no respecter of persons. He calls everyone, and those who believe in Christ as his only begotten Son are given to Jesus."

People reject the concept of being "Born Again" for various reasons, and these can be deeply personal. Here are some common reasons:

- **Misunderstanding or Lack of Awareness**: Some individuals may not fully understand what it means to be "Born Again." They might associate it with religious rituals or legalistic requirements rather than a genuine spiritual transformation.

- **Intellectual Skepticism**: People with a skeptical mindset may question the idea of spiritual rebirth. They might find it difficult to accept supernatural concepts without empirical evidence.

- **Fear of Change**: Being "Born Again" implies a radical shift in one's life. It requires surrendering control and embracing God's plan. Some people fear this change and prefer to remain in their comfort zones.

- **Negative Experiences With Religion**: Past negative experiences within religious institutions or with religious leaders can lead to rejection. Hurtful encounters, hypocrisy, or legalism can create a barrier to accepting spiritual truth.

- **Worldly Attachments**: Materialism, worldly desires, and attachments can hinder openness to spiritual matters. The pursuit of pleasure, success, or self-centered goals may overshadow the need for spiritual rebirth.

- **Pride And Self-Reliance**: Pride can prevent someone from acknowledging their need for salvation. Believing they can achieve righteousness on their own, they reject the idea of being "Born Again" through faith in Christ.

- **Moral Relativism**: In a culture that promotes moral relativism, some people reject absolute truth. They may view the concept of being "Born Again" as narrow-minded or exclusive.

- **Emotional Barriers**: Past trauma, emotional

wounds, or unresolved issues can create emotional barriers. Accepting spiritual rebirth may require addressing these underlying hurts.

- **Peer Pressure And Social Acceptance**: Fear of rejection by peers or society can influence a person's decision. Choosing to be "Born Again" may set them apart from their social circles.

- **Spiritual Warfare**: The Bible speaks of spiritual forces opposing God's truth. These unseen battles can influence a person's receptivity to the gospel message.

It is essential to approach these reasons with empathy and understanding. Encouraging open dialogue and sharing personal testimonies can help bridge the gap and lead people toward the transformative experience of being "Born Again." (Excerpts from Odyssey)

As I see it, ***the major reason*** folks reject being "Born Again" is they do not believe in the fall of man from God's grace. Romans 5:12 clearly shows what happened. It says,

"Wherefore, as by one man sin entered into the world, and death by sin; and so death passed upon all men, for that all have sinned."

Sin entered the world by the disobedience of Adam and passed on to his descendants. The sin was a willful rejection of God's will…an attitude of rebellion that caused every descendent of Adam to also sin. No one could escape this evil nature that came from Satan through Adam. Thus, people reject being "Born Again" because they are in a state of rebellion all the time and care not about God's grace. They are too busy being their own god.

Regardless of what others believe or do, we seek Jesus and we find him in the "Looking Glass," which is the Bible.

CHAPTER TWO:
SEEING YOURSELF IN THE LOOKING GLASS

What do you see when you look in the mirror? Is it that old man or woman that frowns, is grumpy and full of attitudes? Or is it the new creature adorned with the glory of the Lord?

Paul is telling the church folks that it is a mystery. Remember, the looking glass is a mirror where we can see ourselves and the new creature at the same time. It is a metaphor for the Bible.

When I first read the Bible (Looked into the looking glass), here is what I saw:

- And you, being dead in your sins and the uncircumcision of your flesh, has he quickened together with him, having forgiven you all trespasses; Colossians 2:13.

- For all have sinned, and come short of the glory of

God; 24 Being justified freely by his grace through the redemption that is in Christ Jesus: Romans 3:23-24.

- For the wages of sin is death, but the free gift of God is eternal life in Christ Jesus, our Lord. Romans 6:23.

- For God so loved the world, that he gave his only be-gotten Son, that whosoever believeth in him should not perish, but have everlasting life. John 3:16.

What I saw in the Bible was depressing. I was myself as lost and dead in my sins. I fell short of God's glory. I had earned a sentence of death by my works of sin. I was not alone, all have sinned.

I was also a "Whosoever" that believed and was given the free gift of salvation…eternal life. This gave me hope and a desire to change.

Paul goes on to say, "we are changed into the same image from glory to glory and it is the Spirit of the Lord that causes the changes… even as by the Spirit of the Lord" Let's break this out into points.

- When we look into a mirror, which is a metaphor for the Bible, we should be seeing the Glory of the Lord.

- When we do this, we are to come to the mirror with an "Open Face", meaning with no veil over our face and free of any attitudes, so we can see the image of God.

- Every time we look, we change (From Glory to Glory)…Each glorious experience changes us… more of Jesus and less of us.

- When we look into the glass, we see the same image over and over again…that of Jesus, for it is the spirit that shows us…but that's not all.

- The Bible is the looking glass where we see Jesus and ourselves.

- We can be sinners seeking to be our own gods or it can be children of God, seeking to glorify Jesus and walk in the Spirit of the living God.

- Usually, we will see us, as the natural man apart from God and as saints, saved by grace. We seek more of Jesus and less of us.

This process of change is not a new concept. Hear the words of Paul again as he writes to the church in Rome. It is recorded in Romans chapter eight.

29. For whom he did foreknow, he also did predestinate *to be* conformed to the image of his Son, that he might be the firstborn among many brethren.

30. Moreover whom he did predestinate, them he also called: and whom he called, them he also justified: and whom he justified, them he also glorified.

31.What shall we then say to these things? If God *be* for us, who *can be* against us? Romans 8:29-31

Again, when we look into the looking glass, we are changed into the image of our creator. We will explore this concept in more detail in chapter three.

The Veil

Do You remember reading about the time when Moses came down from the mountain with the 10- commandments? (The beginning of the Mosaic Law) His face was so bright with the glory of the Lord that the people had to cover his face. They could not look into it. Paul tells us that when we look into the looking glass, we look into the glory of the Lord without being blinded. We need no covering over our heads.

There is a contrast between law and grace and condemnation and forgiveness. The law was given to condemn sin, and as a result, brought death. Grace came by Jesus to provide reconciliation and life.

The implication is clear. We no longer have to fear death because God's grace, in and through Christ, has given us life.

The death of Christ on the cross paid the penalty for our dishonesty or sin. It opened the door for us to repent or renounce the hidden things in our lives that are dishonest. We have the chance of ending up with a clear conscience or "Open Face" as Paul describes it. We cannot behold the glory of the Lord without it.

What do you see when you look in the mirror?

CHAPTER THREE:
THE DOCTRINE
OF CHANGE

The scripture teaches the doctrine of change. Jesus does not change, but we change into his image. We also see this doctrine in Paul's letter to the church in Rome.

"I beseech you therefore, brethren, by the mercies of God, that ye present your bodies a living sacrifice, holy, acceptable unto God, which is your reasonable service. And be not conformed to this world: but be ye transformed by the renewing of your mind, that ye may prove what is that good, and acceptable, and perfect, will of God." **Romans 12:-1-2**

"For I say, through the grace given unto me, to every man that is among you, not to think of himself more highly than he ought to think; but to think soberly, according as God has dealt to every man the measure of faith."

(V.3) Not to think of ourselves is to come with an open face.

You, Me, And The Mirror

Beholding as in a glass is a reference to a looking glass or mirror. I believe that there are two thoughts here.

The first is as a regular mirror, but the second is, in my opinion, as mentioned before, a metaphor for the Bible. It is a mirror for our souls where we see ourselves as we really are. Here are some scriptures that prove my point:

- "All we, like sheep, have gone astray; we have turned everyone to his own way; and the LORD has laid on him the iniquity of us all." **Isaiah 53:6**
- Here we see ourselves as sheep that have lost their perspective.
- "For all have sinned, and come short of the glory of God" **Romans 3:23**

If all have sinned, then we are all sinners. This is revealed to us that we may know who we are without Christ, as we look into the looking glass.

- "I beseech you therefore, brethren, by the mercies of God, that ye present your bodies a living sacrifice, holy, acceptable unto God, which is your reasonable service. **Romans 12:1**

We are buried with him in baptism and raised with him in newness of life.

- "Therefore, if any man be in Christ, he is a new creature: old things are passed away; behold, all things are become new." **II Corinthians 5:17**

A new creation is different than what we are now. We see the new creation that we are becoming as we study the Bible.

- "And have made us unto our God kings and priests: and we shall reign on the earth" … **Rev. 5:10**

A look at our destiny. This is a great future, don't you think?

- "And the LORD shall make thee the head, and not the tail; and thou shalt be above only, and thou shalt not be beneath; if that thou hearken unto the commandments of the LORD thy God, which I command thee this day, to observe and to do them: **Deut. 28-13**

We have God's promise that we will lead, not follow, if we obey the voice of the lord.

I am sure you can find many more examples where the scriptures reflect when we were with Jesus and without Christ.

The point is…as we read the Bible; we see ourselves in various stages of growth…from glory unto glory. We are ever changing into the image of Christ. However, we do not want to be like the man that James spoke of in his letter to the church.

- "For if any be a hearer of the word, and not a doer, he is like unto a man beholding his natural face in a glass: For he beholds himself, and goes his way, and straightway forgets what manner of man he was." **James 1:23-24**

The changing you is dependent upon being a doer of the Word. If you just look into the looking glass and do not apply what you read, you forget it all about the manner of man that you were and what God wanted you to be.

Glory In The Looking Glass

The more you read the Bible, the more you will see Jesus. As you see him, you will also see his Glory…that of the only begotten Son of God. He is like no other man in all of history. This is where you learn of him and develop a relationship. This is where he will speak to your need and direct your steps.

CHAPTER FOUR:
JESUS PICTURED IN THE LOOKING GLASS

Take a look into the looking glass. Here are a few things you will see regarding Jesus.

1. The LORD is my shepherd. I shall not want. **Psalm 23:1**

2. Jesus said to them, "I am the bread of life; he who comes to me will not hunger, and he who believes in me will never thirst. "But I said to you that you have seen me, and yet do not believe. "All that the Father gives me will come to me, and the one who comes to me I will certainly not cast out. *John 6:36-51*

3. Then Jesus again spoke to them, saying, "I am the light of the world; he who follows me will not walk in the darkness, but will have the Light of life." *John 8:12*

4. The next day John saw Jesus coming toward him and

said, "Behold, the Lamb of God", who takes away the sin of the world! *John 1:29*

5. Revelation 5:5: And one of the elders saith unto me, Weep not: behold, the Lion of the tribe of Judah, the Root of David, has prevailed to open the book, and to lose the seven seals thereof. *Revelation 5:5*

Again, I am sure you will see other descriptions of Christ as you gaze into the looking glass. Just in these few examples, we have seen Jesus as a Lion, a Lamb, the Light of the world, and our Shepherd. We do not want to overlook him as our Savior.

"For if, while we were God's enemies, we were reconciled to him through the death of his Son, how much more, having been reconciled, shall we be saved through his life!" *Romans 5:10* **NIV** There is more…take a look and see.

I know that I found the Lord as I studied the scriptures. I saw him and watched, as if I was watching a movie. I also heard his voice spoken to others in his earthly days and me in these last days. As I read the scriptures, the words leaped off the pages right into my heart.

I even saw myself changing as I experienced divine revelations of truth, faith, and perspective. It is all in the looking glass, waiting for us to gaze upon the mysteries, and feel the joy of life in relationship with God.

CHAPTER FIVE:
THE EVER CHANGING YOU

The beautiful picture that emerges in the looking glass, as you continually gaze into it, is an ever changing you. It is almost like a caterpillar that goes through metamorphism to eventually become a new creature…the butterfly. From glory to glory, slow but steady, as we read and apply God's Word, we are changed into the very image of Christ.

This is the mystery of the looking glass. People will see you and they will see you and they will also see God's image. They will see his image growing brighter and brighter as you look into the looking glass.

The pattern of unrighteousness gives way to righteousness, not ours, but the righteousness of Christ.

"For he made him who knew no sin to be sin for us, that we might become the righteousness of God in him." **II Corinthians 5:21**

The fallen nature of man, with its deeds of immorality, suddenly cones into conflict with the fruit of God's Spirit that grows to maturity as we gaze into the looking glass.

 "But the fruit of the Spirit is love, joy, peace, longsuffering, kindness, goodness, faithfulness, gentleness, self-control. Against such, there is no law. And those who are Christ's have crucified the flesh with its passions and desires." **Galatians 5:22-24**

We now have a choice and the where-with-all to overcome the evil that resides inside of us. The old heart & spirit are taken away and replaced with the new creature in Christ.

 "A new heart also will I give you, and a new spirit will I put within you: and I will take away the stony heart out of your flesh, and I will give you an heart of flesh." ***Ezekiel 36:26***

As a result of beholding God's Glory in the looking glass (The Bible), we are "being transformed" "being changed" The verb is *metamorphoō*, "to change inwardly in fundamental character or condition, be changed, be Transformed." It is a compound verb, formed from *meta-*, "exchange, transfer, transmutation" + *morphoō*, "to form, shape." From this we get our English word "metamorphosis.

Paul is also using the looking glass to show the transformation from the Law to Grace. It eventually changes, as does its foundation upon which we stand. Our salvation now is in Jesus, not the Law of Moses. He made this clear in **Galatians 3:1-3** when he said…

"O foolish Galatians, who has bewitched you, that ye should not obey the truth, before whose eyes Jesus Christ has been evidently set forth, crucified among you? This only would I learn of you, received ye the Spirit by the works of the law, or by the hearing of faith? Are ye so foolish, having begun in the Spirit, are ye now made perfect by the flesh?"

Here in this one scripture, **II Corinthians 3:18**, we can see how God uses his grace as the foundation for salvation and how the believer is justified by faith, not works of the law. God.

However, salvation has always been by grace. The Law made manifest the true nature of man without God. We would never have known it was wrong to steal unless the law said it was wrong. It was a schoolmaster to show us our own depravity, so we would call upon the grace of God to save us.

The law was a picture of righteousness by which man could measure his own holiness. But man could not live the law because he was sinful and by nature fell short of God's glory. He could not restore the image of God in himself. God had to do that and his grace was the way to do it.

The original plan was to make man in his image and likeness. **Genesis 1:26** The process of change brought on by reading God's word (i.e. looking into the looking glass") is our divine destiny.

There are a lot more benefits that come to us as we gaze into the looking glass. These are just a few.

CHAPTER SIX

JOHN GILLS' BIBLE COMMENTARY

I came across John Gills' expository of the Bible, where I found this commentary. Read what he says. It is a little deep into theology, but very interesting.

But We All With Open Face, We are not like Moses, who had a veil on his face; nor like the Jews, who have one on their hearts: "but we all"; not ministers and preachers of the Gospel only, but all believers, whether Jews or Gentiles, greater or lesser believers, who are enlightened by the Spirit of God, and are converted to Christ: "with open face"; which may regard the object beheld, the glory of Christ un-veiled, that has no veil on it, as Moses had on his face, when he delivered the law; or the persons beholding, who are rid of Jewish darkness; the veil of the ceremonial law, and of natural darkness and blindness of mind; and so clearly and fully, comparatively speaking, …

Beholding As In A Glass; Not of the law, but of the Gospel, and the ordinances of it; not with the eyes of their bodies, but with the eyes of their understandings, with the eye of faith; which sight is spiritual, delightful, and very endearing; throws a veil over all other objects and makes souls long to be with Christ: the object beheld is the glory of the Lord;

Jesus Christ: not the glory of his human nature, which lies in its union to the Son of God, and in its names which it has by virtue of it; and in its being the curious workmanship of the Spirit of God, and so is pure and holy, and free from all sin; and was outwardly beautiful and glorious, and is so at the right hand of God, where we see him by faith, crowned with glory and honor; and shall behold him with the eyes of our bodies, and which will be fashioned like to his glorious body; but this sight and change are not yet: rather, the glory of his divine nature is meant, which is essential and underived.

The same with his father's; is ineffable and incomprehensible; it appears in the perfections he is possessed of, and in the worship given to him; it was manifested in the doctrines taught, and in the miracles wrought by him; there were some breakings forth of this glory in his state of humiliation, and were beheld by the apostles and other believers, who saw his glory, as the glory of the only begotten of the Father. Though the glory of Christ as Mediator, being full of grace and truth, seems to be chiefly designed; this he has from God, and had it from everlasting; this he gives to his people, and is what makes him so glorious, lovely, and desirable in their eye: and whilst this delightful object is beheld by them, they are ....

Changed Into The Same Image; there was a divine image

in man, in his first creation; this image was defaced by sin, and a different one took place; now in regeneration, another distinct from them both is stamped, and this is the image of Christ; he himself is formed in the soul, his grace is wrought there; so that it is no wonder there is a likeness between them; which lies in righteousness and holiness, and shows itself in acts of grace and a discharge of duty. The gradual motion of the change into this image is expressed by this phrase, …

From Glory To Glory: not from the glory of the law to the glory of the Gospel; or from the glory of Moses to the glory of Christ; rather from the glory that is in Christ, to a glory derived in believers from him; or which seems most agreeable, from one degree of grace to another, grace here being signified by glory; or from glory begun here to glory perfect hereafter; when this image will be completed, both in soul and body; and the saints will be as perfectly like to Christ, as they are capable of, and see him as he is: now the efficient cause of all this, "is the Spirit of the Lord".

It is he that takes off the veil from the heart, that we may, with open face unveiled, behold all this glory; it is he that regenerates, stamps the image of Christ, and conforms the soul to his likeness; it is he that gradually carries on the work of grace upon the soul, increases faith, enlarges the views of the glory of Christ, and the spiritual light, knowledge, and experience of the saints, and will perfect all that which concerns them; will quicken their mortal bodies and make them like to Christ; and will forever rest as a spirit of glory on them, both in soul and body: some read these words, …

By The Lord of The Spirit, and understand them of Christ, others read them, "by the Lord the Spirit, ", as they very well may be rendered; and so are a proof of the true and proper deity of the Holy Spirit, who is the one Jehovah with the Father and the Son. The ancient Jews owned this; ``the Spirit of the living God, (say F11 they,) (arwbh wnyyh) , this is the Creator himself, from him all spirits are produced; blessed be he, and blessed be his name, because his name is he himself, for his name is Jehovah."

CHAPTER SEVEN

THE IMAGE & LIKENESS OF GOD

A Snapshot Or Facsimile

If we are being changed into the image and likeness of God, just what does that mean? I found an article by Dick Staub of "Relevant Magazine" in March 2003. He gives a good explanation.

All our lives we have heard that we are "made in the image of God." It is a nice thought, and probably one we have clung to when we need a reminder of our own value. But have you ever stopped to think about what it really means? "Made in the image of God" is an audacious claim—and one that probably carries some responsibility with it.

We all know we are not gods—though if we are honest, we know we often think we are the god of our own lives, even if we'd never admit it. The truth is, you are not God. But you are godlike.

Our confusion about whether we are God arises from our

godlikeness. It is described in the first chapter of the Bible. **Genesis 1:26-27** reveals,

"Then God said, 'Let us make man in our image, in our likeness' ... So God created man in his own image, in the image of God he created him; male and female, he created them."

To be fully human is to fully reflect God's creative, spiritual, intelligent, communicative, relational, moral, and purposeful capacities.

So, what does it mean to be created in God's image? The Hebrew root of the Latin phrase for image of God—*imago Dei*—means image, shadow, or likeness of God. You are **a snapshot** or **facsimile** of God. At the very least, this means humans occupy a higher place in the created order because we alone are imprinted with godlike characteristics.

Your godlikeness is the path to your greatest fulfillment. You will feel the greatest pleasure and wholeness when who God made you to be is fully developed and expressed.

Your godlikeness can also be a pitfall, because in our hubris we often confuse being like God with being God. Mystery writer Nevada Barr learned this after returning to faith from her long sojourn on the wild side and concluded: "It was a number of years of crashing and burning before I made the

discovery that I was not God. Finally, I realized that though I was not God, I was of God."

Godlike Aptitudes

But in what way are you an image of God? How are you godlike? Theologians have long debated this question, but the answer becomes clear when we read the description of God in Genesis 1 and then ask: If we could take a snapshot of God, what would we see and what would it reveal about humans created in God's image?

First, the truth about you is that you are creative because God is creative.

"In the beginning God created the heavens and the earth" *(Genesis 1:1).*

We know that God is creative with paint. Poets, writers, philosophers, and lawyers make things with ideas and the compelling use of words. Doctors make people healthier; consultants make organizations better. Manufacturers make things with raw materials; chefs make things with fruits, vegetables, meats, and spices. Every human has the capacity to make things, to create, because we are all made in the image of a creative God.

The **second** truth about you is that you are spiritual because God is Spirit: "The Spirit of God was hovering over the waters" **(Genesis 1:2).** Every human possesses spiritual aptitudes and capacities. We are more than the sum of our physical parts. Our spiritual nature, though unseen, is as real as our physical nature. Nurturing our spirit is as important as eating, drinking, and exercising are to our physical body. Every human makes things. Artists make things.

The very essence of God is relational, and that essential quality has been imprinted on humans.

A **third** truth about you is that you communicate because God communicates: "God said, 'Let there be light'" **(Genesis 1:3).** Anthropologists agree that the emergence of symbolic language—first spoken, then written—represents the sharpest break between animals and humans. The human ability to think and reason, to use language, symbols, and art, far surpasses the abilities of any animals. This gift was bestowed when the communicative God's image was imprinted on us.

A **fourth** truth about you is that you are intelligent because God is intelligent: "In the beginning was the Word [*logos*, a Greek word meaning reason, or logic and "the Word was with God, and the Word was God" **(John 1:1).**

Logical sequential thought flows from the orderliness of God's mind. As a result, though we are not all intellectuals, we each possess a mind and a way of thinking and learning, so Jesus commanded us to love God with our minds (as well as our hearts and all our strength). Because of God's intelligent image imprinted on our lives, though we possess different kinds of intelligence, each of us is to develop our mental capacities to their fullest.

A **fifth** truth about you is that you are relational because God is relational: "Let us make man in our image, in our likeness. ... It is not good for man to be alone" *(Genesis 1:26, Genesis 2:18).* The phrase,

"Let us make man in our image" reveals an "us- ness" in

the very nature of God. The very essence of God is relational, and that essential quality has been imprinted on humans. This capacity for a relationship with God extends to humans, which is why the Genesis story declares that God created Eve for Adam because "it is not good for man to be alone."

NOTE: All these qualities are imprinted on mankind and can easily be seen in our society through those who have applied themselves. However, we must not forget that the spiritual aspect that was once connected between man and God was broken by sin and is in need of restoration.

That is why Jesus came and why we now, with unveiled faces, can gaze into the looking glass of God's Word and be changed by it from glory to glory by his Holy Spirit.

Reading the Bible puts us on the right road where we can ever so slowly or ever so fast become more like Jesus until folks around us begin to see his reflection.

CHAPTER EIGHT:
THE MAKING OF A MAN

I also thought I would share an article from Got/Questions. com on "What It Means To Be Made In The Image of God." I like all of what they say, and you will get a little more detail. It should expand your overall perspective.

On the last day of creation, God said, "Let us make man in our image, in our likeness" (Genesis 1:26). Thus, he finished his work with a "personal touch." God formed man from the dust and gave him life by sharing his own breath (Genesis 2:7). Accordingly, man is unique among all God's creations, having both a material body and an immaterial soul/spirit.

Having the "image" or "likeness" of God means, in the simplest terms, that we were made to resemble God. Adam did not resemble God in the sense of God having flesh and blood.

Scripture says that "God is Spirit" (John 4:24) and therefore exists without a human body. However, Adam's body did mirror the life of God, insofar as, it was created in perfect health and was not subject to death.

The image of God refers to the immaterial part of man. It sets man apart from the animal world, fits him for the dominion God intended him to have over the earth (Genesis 1:28), and enables him to commune with his Maker. It is a likeness mentally, morally, and socially. (*These attributes, added to the fruit of the Spirit, make man's resemblance of God complete.*)

Mentally, man was created as a rational, volitional agent. In other words, man can reason and man can choose. This is a reflection of God's intellect and freedom. Anytime someone invents a machine, writes a book, paints a landscape, enjoys a symphony, calculates a sum, or names a pet, he or she is proclaiming the fact that we are made in God's image.

Morally, man was created in righteousness and perfect innocence, a reflection of God's holiness. God saw all he had made (mankind included) and called it "very good" (Genesis 1:31). Our conscience or "moral compass" is a vestige of that original state. Whenever someone writes a law, recoils from evil, praises good behavior, or feels guilty, he is confirming the fact that we are made in God's own image.

Socially, man was created for fellowship. This reflects God's triune nature and his love. In Eden, man's primary relationship was with God (Genesis 3:8 implies fellowship with God), and God made the first woman because "it is not good for the man to be alone" (Genesis 2:18). Every time someone marries, makes a friend, hugs a child, or attends church, he is demonstrating the fact that we are made in the likeness of God.

Part of being made in God's image is that Adam had the capacity to make free choices. Although he was given a righteous nature, Adam made an evil choice to rebel against his Creator. In so doing,

Adam marred the image of God within himself, and he passed that damaged likeness on to all his descendants (Romans 5:12). Today, we still bear the image of God (James 3:9), but we also bear the scars of sin. Mentally, Morally, Socially, and Physically, we show the effects of sin.

The good news is that when God redeems an individual, he begins to restore the original image of God, creating a "new self", created to be like God in true righteousness and holiness. (Ephesians 4:24). That redemption is only available by God's grace through faith in Jesus Christ as our Savior from the sin that separates us from God (Ephesians 2:8-9). Through Christ, we are made new creations in the likeness of God (2 Corinthians 5:17).

This is all done gradually as we gaze into the looking glass, which is God's Word.

CHAPTER NINE:
LAW AND GRACE EXPLAINED

I do not want you to miss the central theme of Paul's teaching. He wanted the 1st century Christians to be clear on the foundation of their salvation. I also feel the need to be sure you have the truth so you can stand against all the deception and lies in our religious community.

The Old Testament saints trusted in the "Law of Moses." It was their foundation upon which they could stand in this world and share the hope of eternal life. As discussed previously, the Law had its own glory, but it also came with a veil that hid its glory from the believers. They could not look at the Law and see God. They instead saw his condemnation because they fell short of keeping that which was contained in it.

The hidden truth of the Old Testament was that the Law was never intended to be a foundation for salvation. No one could be or now is able to keep all the law. As Paul said, it was a schoolmaster, given to teach us that we were not our own gods; not perfect; not able to be righteous, like

God is righteous; and are in real need of a Savior. The Law exposed sin. Thou shalt not kill exposed killing as being wrong.

The remedy given by God before the foundation of the world was grace or unmerited favor. John 3:16 tells the story.

"For God so loved the world, that he gave his only begotten Son, that whosoever believeth in him should not perish, but have everlasting life."

Notice there is no mention of keeping the Law, good works, or anything else but belief. The Biblical definition says believe is to rely upon, adhere to and trust in. That is much more than just acknowledging the existence of Jesus in history.

John 3:16 was spoken by Jesus, the Christ, who proved he was the Son of God. Christ is a Greek word for "Anointed One." The Hebrew word for "Anointed One" is Messiah. All the way back in Genesis, when God spoke to the serpent, and said that there would be an "Anointed One" coming in history that would destroy him and his rule over man.

Salvation has always been by grace through faith, first to the Old Testament saints that looked ahead to the coming Messiah and in these last days to the New Testament saints that look back to the cross and trusted in the Christ. Jesus fit the bill for both the Messiah and the Christ. He is the only begotten Son of God.

Paul tells us that the glory of the Law could never match or exceed the glory of Christ and that we must hang out hats on the gospel of grace, not works of righteousness, because the righteousness of Christ given in the new covenant far exceeds the old covenant.

The new covenant established by Jesus fulfilled the righteousness of the old covenant, thereby abolishing it. No longer did folks have to keep the Law to be righteous. Jesús did that for us. Our righteousness is secured in him and his life.

CHAPTER TEN:
APPLIED CRUCIFIXION

Just what does it mean to follow Jesus? If we follow him, where is he going? Most 1ˢᵗ century Christians knew the answers, counted the cost, and still became disciples.

The cost was to die to themselves. Their own crucifixion was the cost of discipleship. They had to die to their own will and accept the will of God. Only then could Jesus bring forth his image in them.

I struggled for years to figure out how I could die and still live. If I die to myself, am I still here? Where did I go and where is Jesus?

Finally, one day, I realized what it all meant. That which is pictured in the process of change seen in the "Looking Glass" is actually *Applied Crucifixion*. Here is a scripture to support my reasoning:

"And they that are Christ's have crucified the flesh with the affections and lusts." Galatians 5:24

The teaching is by Paul in a letter to the Galatians. He did not mean we literally would perish so Jesus could have our bodies to live out his life.

What he is saying is that those that follow Jesus actively deny the works of the flesh that are alive in all of us. They are the nature of the natural man without Christ.

Paul listed the major works of the flesh. "Now the works of the flesh are manifest, which are these; Adultery, fornication, uncleanness, lasciviousness, Idolatry, witchcraft, hatred, variance, emulations, wrath, strife, seditions, heresies, envying, murders, drunkenness, revellings, and such like: of the which I tell you before, as I have also told you in time past, that they which do such things shall not inherit the kingdom of God." Galatians 5:19-21.

Denying theses bad things access to rule over our lives, refusing to act upon suggestions to participate in them is what I call, "Applied Crucifixion" We kill them before they take root.

You may be asking, "How so?" We kill them by walking in the Spirit. Let's take wrath. To stop its active manifestation, we walk in peace and show kindness.

Here's what Paul list of the fruit of the Spirit:

"But the fruit of the Spirit is love, joy, peace, longsuffering, gentleness, goodness, faith, Meekness, temperance: against such there is no law. And they that are Christ's have crucified the flesh with the affections and lusts. If we live in the Spirit, let us also walk in the Spirit." Galatians 5:22-25

I can use gentleness against anger or faith against doubt. I can walk in longsuffering to overcome problems. How about using peace to overcome anxiety?

When you walk in the Spirit, you engage the fruit; it kills the work of the flesh and allows the Spirit to manifest the image of God as explained in the looking glass. This is no more than self-denial. You cannot be in both places at the same time. You either walk in the flesh or in the Spirit.

Thank God we have "Free Will." We can select, by our fee will choices, to walk in the Spirit. The two choices we have are God's Spirit or the spirit of Satan. There is no middle ground. There is no neutral place where we can just do our own thing. God created us to be in his image. It is our destiny and why we are given the "Looking Glass" to see and experience that reality.

They that are Christ's have selected to walk in his Spirit and by doing so have crucified the flesh with the affections and lust thereof. They are no longer slaves to sin. They can overcome and be free to serve the Lord.

CONCLUSION

We can now see the glory of God. There is no veil obscuring our vision. As we read the pages of the Bible, which is God's looking glass, it changes us. Our attitudes change. Our thinking really changes. Our actions become more like what God would do. We become that "New creature" spoken of in the scriptures.

"Therefore, if any man be in Christ, he is a new creature: old things are passed away; behold, all things are become new." II Corinthians 5:17.

Old things really do pass away, and new things take their place.

We end up seeing ourselves with a special anointing that brings the righteousness of God to our souls and sets our spirits free from the bondage of sin and death. How great is that?

Now look in the mirror of God's Word. What do you see? You should be seeing Jesus. You should also be seeing yourself as a "New Creature". You should not see "Old Things" because they are or have passed away, no longer to be remembered.

When you realize that your destiny is to be like Jesus, you will be faced with a decision. It is the biggest decision of your life. Will you allow God to change you into the reflection of his dear Son? Or will you continue to build your own self-absorbed life that excludes God and leads to eternal damnation?

Life is too short to waste it on foolish things that die with you. Maybe it is time to gaze into the "Looking Glass" and see what God has in store for you. The decision is yours, but beware, your eternal destiny hangs in the balance.

ABOUT THE AUTHOR JOHN MARINELLI

Rev. Marinelli is an ordained minister. He has formed and been pastor of one church in Wisconsin and was the pastor of another in Alabama. He has also been a youth minister and evangelism director over the years.

Rev. Marinelli has authored over 35 books and now offers other Christian writers free counsel and help in publishing their Christian books.

His books and other information on publishing are available for viewing on his website. www.marinellichristianbooks.com

John is an accomplished Christian poet. He dabbles in songwriting and is an accomplished Christian poet.

He is the Vice President of Have A Heart For Companion Animals, Inc., a "No Kill" animal welfare organization. He volunteers his time promoting fundraising events for www. haveaheartusa.org.

Rev. Marinelli spent 35 years in the sales and marketing arena working as a sales manager for several advertising sales companies. He is now retired from business-to-business and non-profit marketing. He enjoys writing Christian themed books, playing chess, singing karaoke, and a blessed lifestyle in sunny Florida.

GALLERY OF ENCOURAGING CHRISTIAN POEMS

AGREEING WITH GOD

We speak of things that are not,
Believing in them as though they were,
Because our Heavenly Father spoke them first,
Sending them to us in promises that never blur.

We take Him at His Word,
And listen to all He has to say.
We wrap each promise around our souls,
Until what was spoken becomes our day.

We will agree with the Lord,
Trusting that He knows best.
For only His awesome power,
Can provide our souls with rest.

"As it is written, I have made thee a father of many nations, before Him who he believed, even God who quickens the dead and calls those things that be not as though they were" Romans 4:17

Like Abraham, we also have a destiny that God has spoken into our lives. He calls it forth before it exists. Like Abraham, we are to believe, even against hope, that what God said will indeed come to be. (Romans 4:18).

ARM'S LENGTH

I hold the world at arm's length,
That its choices do not interfere.
While it does its own thing,
I watch and wait over here.

My steps must not go that way,
For it's not where I need to be.
The Lord has shown me the path,
That will lead me to my destiny.

The call of the world is strong
And pulls at me now and then.
But I know that way
Is full of sorrow and sin.

I must move on in life
Beyond their beckoning call.
It's the right thing to do,
So I do not stumble or fall.

I will not be swayed or misled
By family, friends or business deal.
Their secret thoughts are not mine,
To consider, to admire or feel.

So I keep the world at "Arm's Length"
As I journey through this life.
My faith in Jesus keeps me strong,
As I walk in His glorious light.

"Love not the world, neither the things that are in the world. If any man loves the world, the love of the Father is not in him. For all that is in the world, the lust of the flesh, the lust of the eyes and the pride of life, is not of the Father, but of the world. And the world passes away and the lust thereof: But he that doeth the will of God abides forever. I John 2:15-17

It is more important to know God and to follow after Him, than to become entangled in life's lustful traps: for if we were to gain the whole world and lose our own soul, how terrible would that be?

DON'T WORRY

Don't worry about tomorrow.
You did that yesterday.
Go on with your life
And remember always to pray.

Ask and it shall be given to you,
But this great truth you already know.
Rejoice and be happy, why? Because…
Your harvest comes from what you sow.

I will say it again and even more,
Until it becomes very very clear.
Tomorrow will take care of itself,
But worry is another word for fear.

Now here's what I want you to do.
Trust in the Lord and be of good cheer.
Drop the worry from your vocabulary
And cast out that demon of fear.

Worry is the flipside of faith. If you are walking in faith, you are free from worry. Why, because faith hopes in God and trusts that he will be there to meet your need.

TWO HOUSES

We built our homes together,
Mine upon a Rock and his in the sand.
He thought his would be all right,
But he was a foolish man.

God's wisdom showed me the way.
And what I needed to do,
But my foolish neighbor,
Never had a clue.

Then the rains came,
And the winds began to blow.
The storms beat upon our homes,
And we had nowhere to go.

We built our homes together,
My neighbor and me.
Mine is still there upon the Rock,
But his ceased to be.

Wise men and fools both suffer,
The storms that befall mankind.
But those who trust in Jesus
Will always stand the test of time.

Foundation is everything. If you build your life on the Word of God, it will last forever. That's why we strive to be obedient to the will of God. We want his destine and his blessings, no matter what the world system thinks or does.

CLUTTER

Clutter keeps the mind confused,
As images dance through the night.
Lost among those unimportant thoughts,
Are the dreams that once shined bright.

An endless parade of fear and doubt,
Crowds the mind to destroy our day.
Ever soaring on the wings of the soul,
Until it has formed an evil array.

But clutter is by one's choice,
Of those who dance to its beat.
Better to face imaginations' due
Than to fall into utter defeat.

Be Quiet!!! Is our spirit's desperate cry,
As we call upon the name of the Lord.
Silence is our heart's desired prayer,
Until our minds are again restored.

"Keep thy heart with all diligence: for out of it are the issues of life" Proverbs 4:23

We make the final choices in life that either lead us astray or closer to the Lord. We chose what enters our hearts and fills our minds. May we always choose the path of righteousness and the way of peace.

THE LORD'S LITTLE
TWO BY FOUR

God has a little 2' X 4'
That rest on heaven's windowsill.
He uses it now and then,
When we stray from His will.

Sometimes we need a good "Bap";
With the Lord's little 2' X 4'
To knock out the confusion,
And help us to desire Him more.

The Lord's little 2' X 4'
Is what we sometimes need,
To get our thinking straight,
And keep our focus indeed.

The Lord's little 2' X 4'
Is fashioned from life's every trial,
So we do not stray from His will,
Or fall into an ungodly lifestyle.

"My son, despise not the chastening of the Lord; neither be weary of His correction: for whom the Lord loves, He corrects; even as a father his son, in whom he delights." Proverbs 3:11 & 12

It is a good thing to be corrected by God. We should not fear His rebuke for it is not His wrath, but rather a blessing from His love that keeps us moving on towards maturity.

I FIND MYSELF IN GOD

I find myself in God.
He is my, "Everything"
I know that He is Lord,
My Life, My Hope, My King.

I find myself in God,
Not the ways of Sin.
Nor do I look to others,
To know who I really am.

I find myself in God,
To whom I bow on bended knee.
He alone is my joy and strength
And where I want to be.

"For we are His workmanship, created in Christ Jesus unto good works, which God hath before ordained, that we should walk in them" Ephesians 2:10

Knowing that we are created in Christ Jesus gives us confidence to walk in Christ, as He walked, along a pathway of good works. It is our joy and pleasure to be like Him. In Him we move and live and have our being.

"I AM" THERE

"I AM" There,
At the end of your broken dreams,
Before the sun rises over your day,
Prior to those tear-filled streams.

"I AM" There,
Down that road of despair,
When all appears to be lost,
And no one seems to care.

"I AM" There,
Over all of life's twists and turns,
When tomorrow is all but gone,
And when you are full of concerns.

"I AM" There,
Sayeth the Lord of Host,
To bring you hope and peace,
And the power of My Holy Ghost.

"I AM" There,
To be sure you make it through,
In the midst of every trial,
To bless your life and deliver you.

"I Am" There

"All power is given unto me in heaven and earth. Go ye therefore and teach all nations, baptizing them in the name of the Father, and of the Son, and of the Holy Ghost: Teaching them to observe all things, whatsoever I have commanded you: and lo, I am with you always, even unto the end of the world." Mathew 28:18-20

The Lord is with us always. He never leaves our side, even when we leave His. In every situation, He is there. It's time to count on His presence and trust in His care.

SO LISTEN UP

I write this verse that all should know.
What I have to say is like a seed, ready to grow.
So listen up to all I have to say.
It could be the very blessing your heart needs today.

God has not given you a spirit of fear.
Instead, He has offered to dry up every tear.
He really loves you, even though you often fail.
His love and mercy follows you,
Enabling you to be the head and not the tail.
So do not worry or even fret.
That's why Jesus paid sin's awful debt.
Now go on in life to discover its victory
Knowing that Jesus has indeed set you free.

"For God hath not given us the spirit of fear: but of Power and of Love and a sound mine" II Timothy 1:7

There is nothing to fear except fear itself and that spirit has been defeated on the cross. We now have the Spirit of power and love and a sound mind. He will never leave us or forsake us. We are truly free.

WINNING THE BATTLE

We must use the Word of God
To calm emotions that fray.
For the enemy never sleeps,
Until he has led us astray.

So when your emotions overflow
With feelings like depression and fear.
Know this! If you dwell in that place,
You invite the enemy to draw near.

When your emotions rage
With fiery darts aglow,
Stand in the power of the Lord,
Against its awful woe.

And if you get confused
And lost in the storm,
Put your thoughts on trial,
Rejecting all but heaven born.

You can win the battle
That rages within your soul.
By casting down imaginations,
And breaking Satan's hold.

Remember to focus on Jesus,
Holding the world at arm's length.
Lift up your head above the trial,
And the Lord will give you strength.

"For the weapons of our warfare are not carnal but mighty, through God, to the pulling down of strongholds: casting down imaginations and every high thing that exalts itself against the knowledge of God, and bringing into captivity every thought to the obedience of Christ." II Corinthians 10:3-5 The battle is in our minds and we win by putting our thoughts on trial and casting out all that oppose the knowledge of God. This is true victory.

THE LIGHTHOUSE

A lighthouse is a blessing,
To the ships that toss in the sea.
For it shows them the way,
Until they can clearly see.

The rage of an angry storm,
Cannot hide its brilliant light.
Nor can its awesome furry,
Rule as an endless night.

Jesus is the lighthouse,
For those who have gone astray.
The light of His love,
Offers a new and living way.
Jesus is the lighthouse,
When fear and sickness rage.
The light of His love,
Gives hope in difficult days.

So trust in the Lord,
And look for His light.
He alone is "The Lighthouse",
That guides you through the night.

"I am the Way, the Truth, and the Life. No man cometh to the Father but by me" John 14:6

Life holds many dark nights that are full of unexpected storms. Only a deep abiding faith in Jesus Christ will get us through. He is the light of the world. His light keeps us from falling into confusion, sorrow, sickness and demonic oppression.

THE WAY MAKER

Only Jesus can make a way,
Through the difficulties of life.
He alone is Lord and King,
Over life's sorrows and strife.

He is the "Way Maker,"
When there is no visible way.
He will make the way known,
As though it were the light of day.

He will make a way,
For those of humble heart.
He will clear away the rubble,
Restoring what Satan broke apart.
Jesus is the "Way Maker,"
A friend to all who are lost.
He has made the way,
Paying sin's incredible cost.

The way to the Maker,
Is through His only Son.
He alone is the "Way Maker,"
Until life's battles are won.

"Let not your heart be troubled. Ye believe in God, believe also in me. In my father's house are many mansions: If it were not so, I would have told you. I go to prepare a place for you. And if I go and prepare a place for you, I will come again, and receive you unto myself, that where I am, there ye may be also." John 14: 1-3

The Lord is prepared for any emergency. He knows the beginning from the end and has gone before us to prepare a way that we can follow until we see Him face to face.

STINKING THINKING

Stinking thinking, they say,
Is bad for your health.
For it frustrates life's goals,
And denies happiness and wealth.

A right perspective is important,
As we think about everything.
It will either bring us down,
Or cause us to shout and sing.

What we think about these days,
Really does affect our life.
It can cause us to overflow with Joy,
Or fall into depression and strife.

So don't let your thinking,
Stink all the way up to heaven.
Stand in faith before God,
And get rid of that negative leaven.

"Then Jesus said unto them, take heed and beware of the leaven of the Pharisees and the Sadducees" Mathew 16:6

Someone once said, "We are what we think" The Bible says, "As a man thinks, so is he" It is important to concentrate our thinking of those things that are of good report, pure, honest and that will keep us clean of heart.

WISE MEN STILL SEEK HIM

Wise men still seek Him
Who appeared so long ago.
They come now by grace
Through faithful hearts aglow.

Wise men still seek Him
For He is their "Bread of Life."
A sustaining inner strength
Through times of sorrow or strife.

Wise men still seek Him
The Christ of Calvary.
God's only begotten Son
Crucified as Sin's penalty.

Wise men still seek Him
Jesus, God in human array.
King of kings & Lord of lords
Born to earth on Christmas Day.

"Now when Jesus was born in Bethlehem of Judea in the days of Herod the king, behold, there came wise men from the east to Jerusalem, saying, where is he that is born king of the Jews? For we have seen his star in the east and are come to worship him" Mathew 2:1-2

Seeking Jesus is the wisest thing any man, woman or child

can do and when we find Him, it is our privilege to bow down and worship Him. This is our journey, our destiny and our life while on this earth.

THE ANGELS CRY HOLY

The Angels cry "Holy,"
While sorrow fills the land.
For God's Judgment Day,
Is to come upon every man.

The Angels cry "Holy,"
While mankind goes astray,
Rejecting the love of God,
To follow his own precarious way.

The Angels cry "Holy,"
Knowing the terror of the Lord,
When all who dwell in sin,
Will suddenly be destroyed.

The Angels cry "Holy,"
Waiting for all things new,
Born of the Holy Spirit,
When God's Judgment is through.

The Angels cry "Holy,"
"Holy is the Lamb,"
Waiting for the children of God,
To join "The Great I AM"

"And one cried unto another and said, "Holy, Holy, Holy, is

the Lord of host: the whole earth is full of his glory" Isaiah 6:3

We serve a Holy God that deserves our reverence and homage. The angels know this and worship Him, but man, because of sin, has no real concept of his own creator.

A HIGHWAY CALLED "HOLINESS"

He places my feet on
A highway called "Holiness,"
That led my soul
To the throne of God.

Amidst the cheers of angels,
I walk, wearing His holy gown.
Onward towards heaven's throne,
While evil cast its awful frown.

My eyes were opened
That I might see.
Both the good and the evil,
That sought after me.

I walk the highway-Holiness
That crosses all of time.
Towards the throne of God,
Leaving this world behind.

"And an highway shall be there, and a way, and it shall be called, the way of holiness; the unclean shall not pass over it; but it shall be for those: the wayfaring men, though fools, shall not err therein. No lion shall be there, nor any ravenous beast shall go up thereon, it shall not be found there, but the redeemed shall walk there. And the redeemed of the Lord shall return, and come to Zion with songs and everlasting joy upon their heads: They shall obtain joy and gladness, and sorrow and sighing shall flee away. " Isaiah 35:8-10

What a privilege to walk the highway of Holiness. It is prepared especially for us, the redeemed, and it is protected from the errors of fools and the snarl of beast and especially the roar of the lion.

CALL UPON THE LORD

When your burdens overwhelm you,
Like a mighty raging sea.
Call upon the Lord, Jesus,
And He will set you free

When your heartaches are many,
And life is difficult to understand.
Call upon the Lord, Jesus.
He will come and hold your hand.

When your friends reject you,
Because you follow after Him,
Call upon the Lord, Jesus.
And keep yourself from sin.

When you fall into depression,
As though it were a giant pit.
Call upon the Lord, Jesus,
Who will restore your joyful wit.

When you're saddened by the day
Feeling lost and all alone.
Call upon the Lord, Jesus,
Who will make His way known.

When you are weary and heavy laden,
Tired from life's many tests.
Call upon the Lord, Jesus,
Who is sure to give you rest.

"Hear my cry; oh God, attend unto my prayer. From the end of the earth, I will cry unto thee, when my heart is overwhelmed: Lead me to the rock that is higher than I." Psalms 61:1-2

Calling upon the Lord in stressful times is o.k. He wants us to cry to Him and then to trust in Him to watch over His Word to perform it on our behalf.

IT CAME TO PASS

Things often come to pass,
But seldom do they ever last.
They come into our busy day,
For awhile, then pass away.

We hear their voices, loud and clear,
As they arrive and while they are here.
They speak both joy and misery,
Some to you and some to me.

We say, "It came to pass,"
Or say, "It happened so fast."
Down life's beaten path,
Comes both love and wrath.

So say goodbye to sad and blue.
To all that is now troubling you.
For things will come, only to pass,
But God's love will always last.

"And it came to pass in those days..." Luke2:1

These are the times of our lives. We live them, some for good and some for not so good. One thing is for sure, that which comes our way, comes only to pass on by. It is not what happens that is so important, but rather what we do with what we are faced with.

Trusting in the Lord and seeking His guidance will always conquer that which comes to pass.

THE WHOSOEVER SCENARIO

The "Whosoever" is who so ever,
Not who so won't, can't or will not.
The story is as clear as a sunny day.
God offers a new and living way.

But only those who engage "free will"
To choose life, faith and obedience,
Will find salvation for their souls,
And be cleansed and made whole.

We do the choosing: to accept or deny.
That is how God set it up to be.
He made the call to life's "Whosoever",
That they could live abundantly.

"For God so loved the world, that he gave his only begotten son, that whosoever believeth in him, should not perish but have everlasting life." John 3:16

We are the "Whosoever" in John 3:16, that one day put his or her faith in Christ, believed in Him and now rest in the Lord's love and grace. We have the promise of God that He sent His Son so we could believe and have everlasting life. How great is that?

LITTLE PRISONS

Little prisons await the man with a lustful soul.
Bars of selfishness and pride create dungeons of icy cold.

Prisons of shame and jealousy fill the
heart with utter despair.
Bars that separate from God and those that really care.

Stand back! While the doors are tightly closed;
Taking away your life, to wither as a dying rose.

Beware of those little prisons that trap the lustful soul.
Keep yourself free from sin through
faith in the Christ of old.

Little prisons need not to be your fate.
It is your choice, Spirit or flesh to date.

"O Foolish Galatians, who hath bewitched you, that ye should not obey the truth, before whose eyes Jesus Christ hath been, evidently set forth, crucified among you? Are you so foolish? Having begun in the Spirit, are you now made perfect in the flesh?

We should always seek to dwell in the Spirit, that we would not emulate the deeds of the flesh. When we fall short, we create "little prisons" that keep us in confusion and away from the blessing of God. It's time to walk in the Spirit and break the prisons that so easily beset us.

A WHISPER IN THE WIND

There's a whisper in the wind
That lingers both day and night.
A champion of truth and justice,
By the power of His might.

A word in due season
That echoes from deep within.
A voice out of nowhere,
Reproving the world of sin.

Look there, in the street
And here, by the shores of the sea.
There's a whisper hidden in the wind;
A voice from eternity.

There's a calling from God.
His voice is hidden in the wind.
In a whisper, He speaks to our hearts
With the love and counsel of a friend.

Listen for the Whisper,
All who seek to know.
It is God's Holy Spirit
Telling you which way to go.

"And thine ears shall hear a word behind thee saying, This

is the way, walk ye in it, when ye turn to the right hand and when ye turn to the left" Isaiah 30:21

The voice of the Lord is often a still small voice, yet always clear and it never brings confusion. His voice is like a whisper in the wind that brings a peaceful breeze to the heart. The joy of hearing His voice is to know His will and our destiny.

FRAGILE FLOWER RED

As a flower in earthen sod,
I bloom for thee, oh God.
To blossom with the turn of spring;
To be to you, a beautiful thing.

I lift my Fragile Flower Red
Upward from my earthen bed;
To draw light from God above,
Strength and peace and joy and love.

As a flower, I bloom for thee
That passersby may stop and see.
Your fragrance and beauty I am,
Flowered in grace as a man.

As a flower in earthen sod,
I bloom for thee, oh God.
Upward, I lift my head,
As a Fragile Flower Red.

"Be not conformed to this world, but be ye transformed, by the renewing of your mind, that ye may prove what is that good and acceptable and perfect will of God."

When we look to God as our source, we blossom, much like a flower that draws light from the sun. When we blossom, like a flower, we display the glory and beauty of our creator to all who care to stop and look. This is our divine destiny.

**Other books by John Marinelli can be viewed and
purchased at:** www.marinellichristianbooks.com

www.ingramcontent.com/pod-product-compliance
Lightning Source LLC
Chambersburg PA
CBHW060442160726
47992CB00003B/1039